ERICCLAPTON
FINGERSTYLE GUITAR COLLECTION

Arranged by Marcel Robinson

ISBN 0-7935-3657-X

HAL•LEONARD™
CORPORATION

7777 W. BLUEMOUND RD. P.O. BOX 13819 MILWAUKEE, WI 53213

This publication is not for sale in
the EC and/or Australia
or New Zealand.

ERIC CLAPTON
INGERSTYLE GUITAR COLLECTION

Badge

Words and Music by Eric Clapton and George Harrison

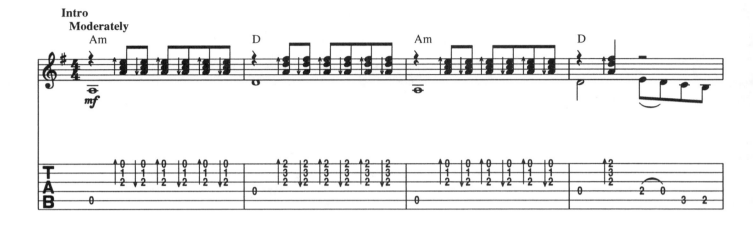

1. Think-in' 'bout the times you drove_ in my car. __
2. I told you not to wan-der 'round_ in the dark. __
3. Talk-in' 'bout a girl that looks_ quite like you. __

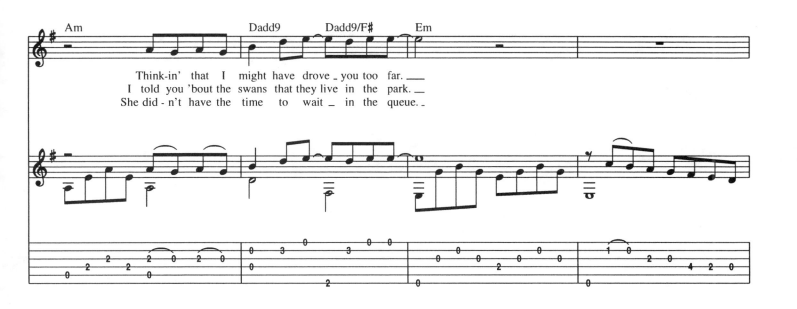

Think-in' that I might have drove _ you too far. __
I told you 'bout the swans that they live in the park. __
She did-n't have the time to wait _ in the queue. __

To Coda ⊕ 1.

And I'm think-in' 'bout the love that you laid on my ta - ble.
Then I told you 'bout the kid. Now he's mar-ried to Ma - bel.
She cried a - way her life since she fell out the cra - dle.

2.

Breakdown

let ring throughout

Bridge

Bell Bottom Blues

Words and Music by Eric Clapton

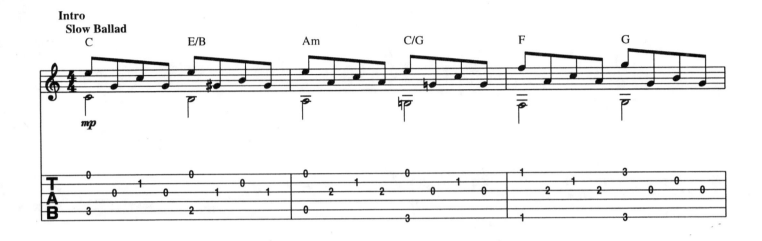

lose this feel - in'. ___
treat me ba - by. ___
meet a - gain. ___

If I could choose ___ a place to
Once I was strong ___ but I lost the
And if we do ___ don't ya be sur -

die, ___
fight; ___
prised. ___

it would be in your ___ arms. ___
you won't find a bet - ter los - er. ___
If you find me with an - oth - er lov - er. ___

Chorus

Do you wan - na see me crawl a - cross the ___

floor to you? ___

Do you wan - na hear me beg you to take me back,

I'd glad - ly do it be - cause

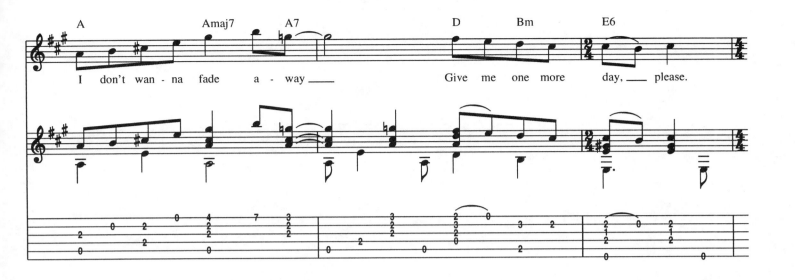

I don't wan-na fade a-way ____ Give me one more day, ____ please.

I don't want to fade a-way. ____ In your heart I want to stay.

1. It's all wrong,
2. Bell Bot - tom

Cocaine

Words and Music by John J. Cale

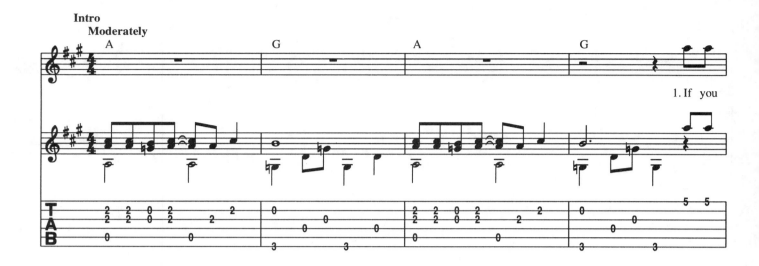

Layla

Words and Music by Eric Clapton and Jim Gordon

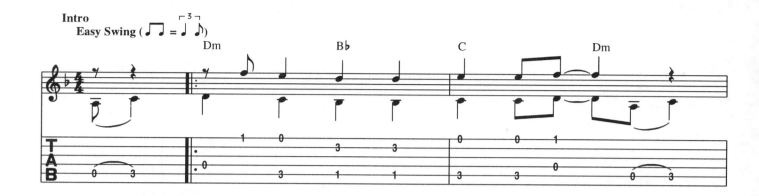

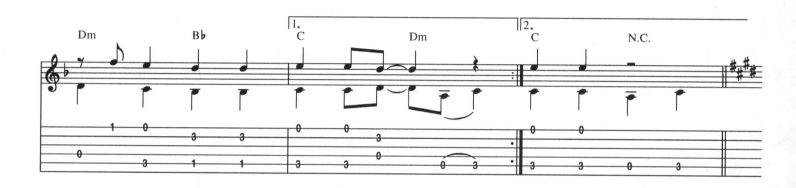

Let it Grow

Words and Music by Eric Clapton

1. Stand-ing at the cross-roads tryin' to read the signs to tell me which way I should go to find the an-swers and

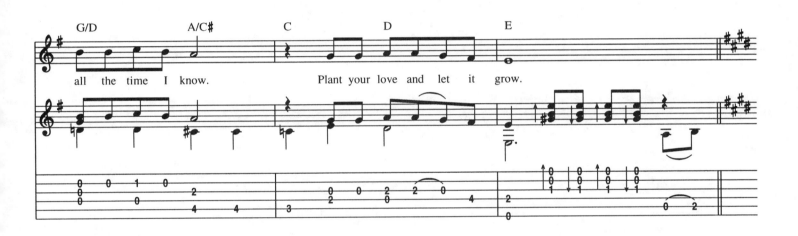

all the time I know. Plant your love and let it grow.

Let it grow, let it grow. Let it blos-som, let it flow.

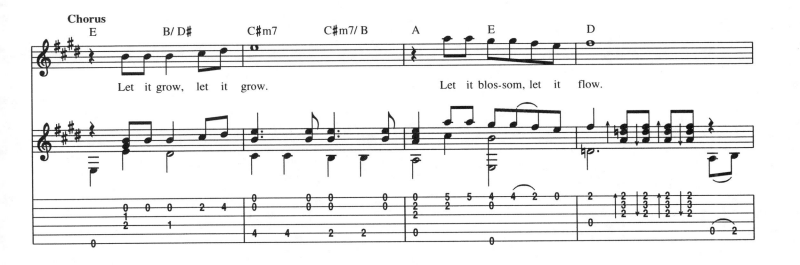

Let it grow, let it grow. Let it blos-som, let it flow.

In the sun, the rain, the snow, love is love - ly. Let it

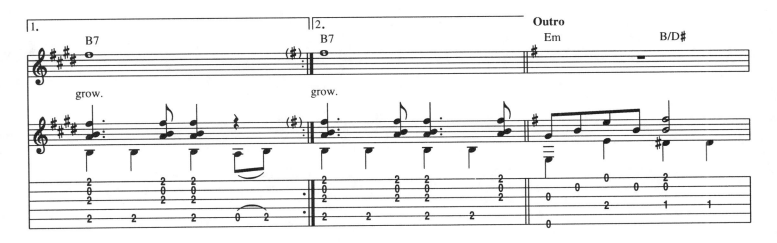

1. grow. 2. grow. **Outro**

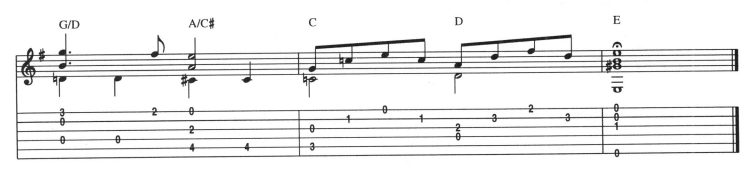

Nobody Knows You
When You're Down And Out

Words and Music by Jimmie Cox

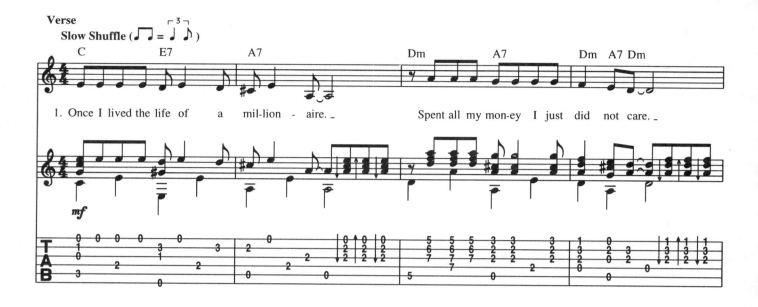

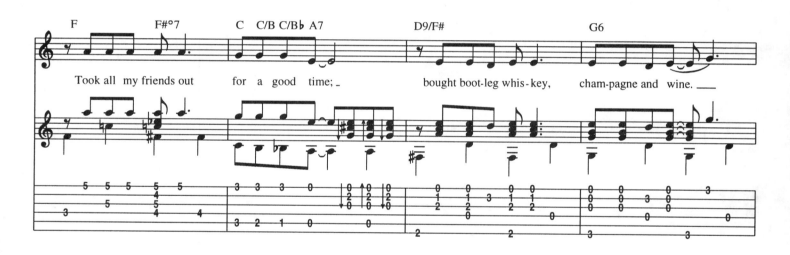

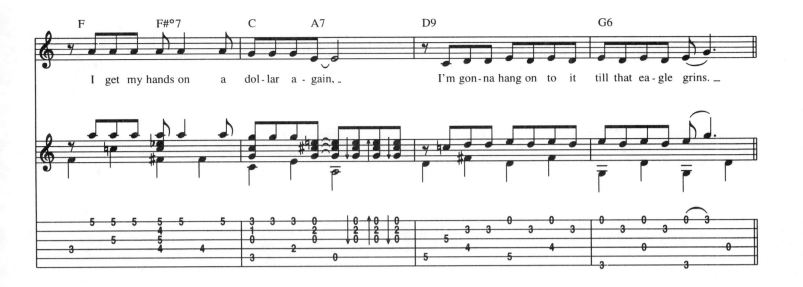

I get my hands on a dol-lar a-gain, _ I'm gon-na hang on to it till that ea-gle grins. _

Chorus

No, no no-bod-y knows you _ when you're down and out. _____

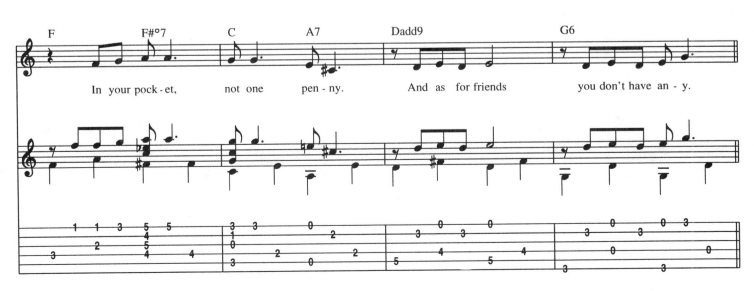

In your pock-et, not one pen-ny. And as for friends you don't have an-y.

Verse

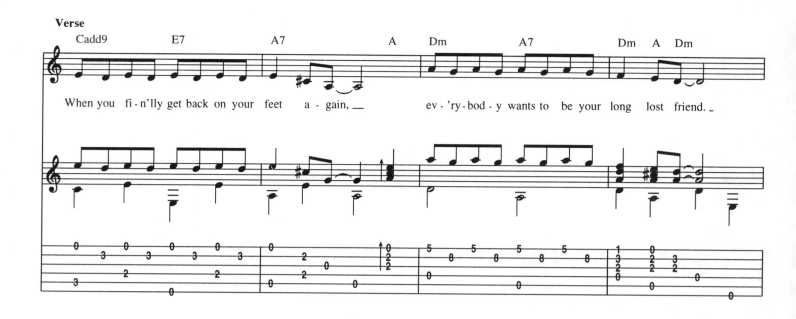

When you fi-n'lly get back on your feet a-gain, __ ev-'ry-bod-y wants to be your long lost friend. __

Said, it's might-y strange, 'out a doubt. __ No-bod-y knows you, no-bod-y knows you

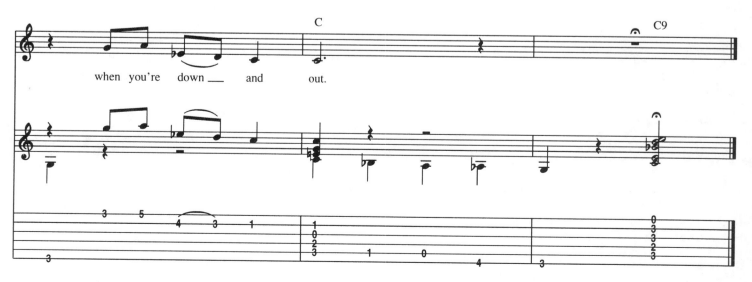

when you're down __ and out.

Tears In Heaven

Words and Music by Eric Clapton and Will Jennings

Running On Faith

Words and Music by Jerry Williams

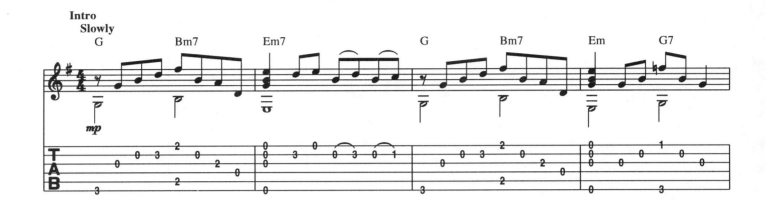

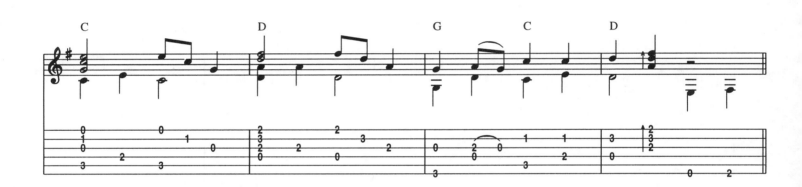

1. Late-ly, I've been run-nin' on faith. Whatelse can a poor boy do? But my
2. Late-ly, I've been talk-in' in my sleep. Can't i - mag-ine what I'd have to say 'cept my

world will be right _ when love comes o - ver you. _
world will be right _ when love comes back your way. _

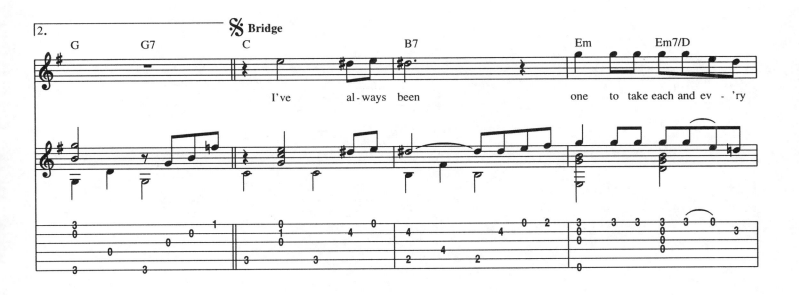

I've al - ways been one to take each and ev - 'ry

day. _ Seems like 'bout now I'd find a love who cares just for

Then we'd go run-nin' on faith. All of our dreams will come

true, and our world would be right when love comes o-ver me and you.

To Coda ⊕

Interlude

26

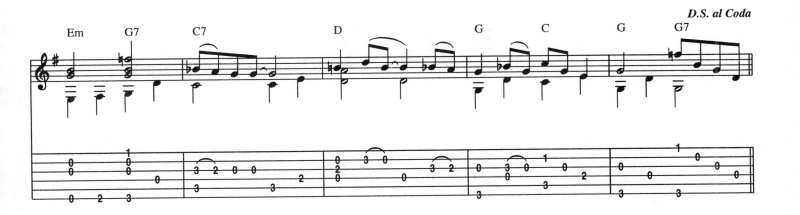

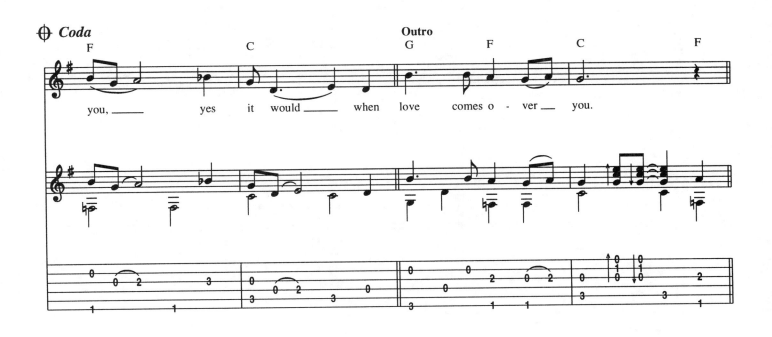

you, _____ yes it would _____ when love comes o - ver _____ you.

Love comes o - ver _____ you.   Love comes o - ver _____ you.

Strange Brew

Words and Music by Eric Clapton, Felix Pappalardi and Gail Collins

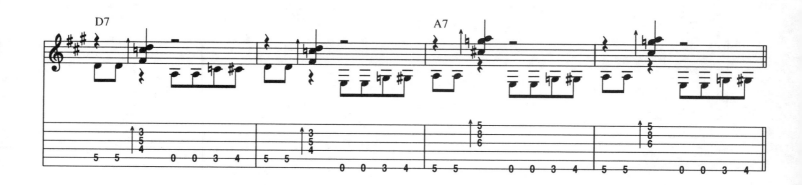

Thorn Tree In The Garden

Words and Music by Bobby Whitlock

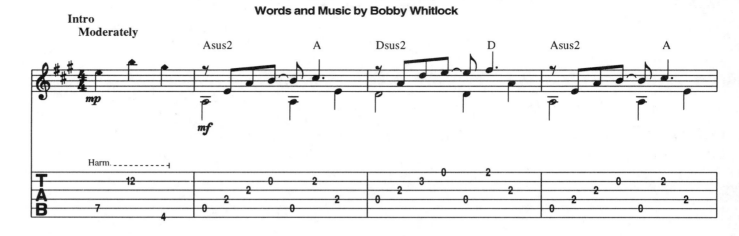

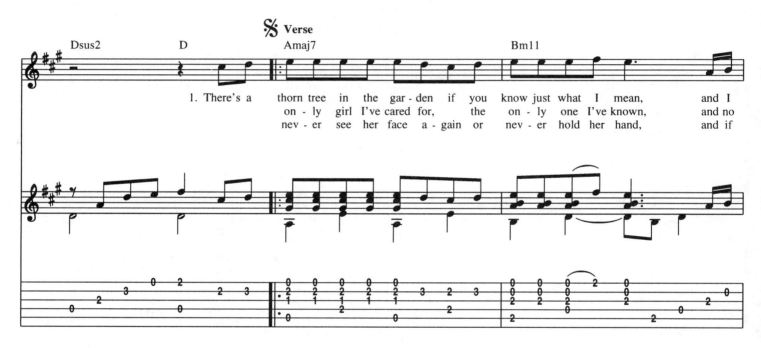

who'll be the one to an-swer why? ___   Lord, I hope it's not __ me.

D.S. al Coda

3. And if I

Coda

White Room

Words and Music by Jack Bruce and Pete Brown

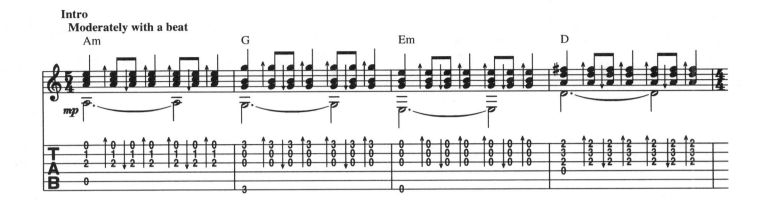

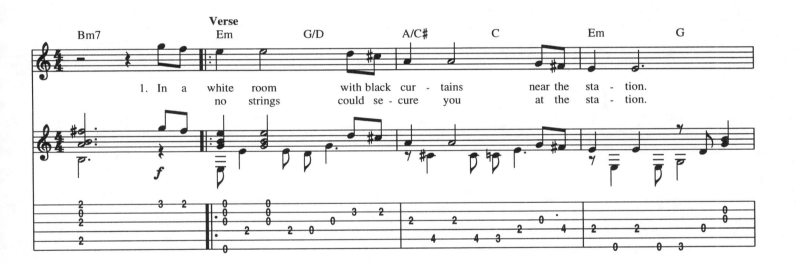

Sil - ver hors - es   run down moon - beams   in your dark eyes.
I walked in - to   such a sad time   at the sta - tion.

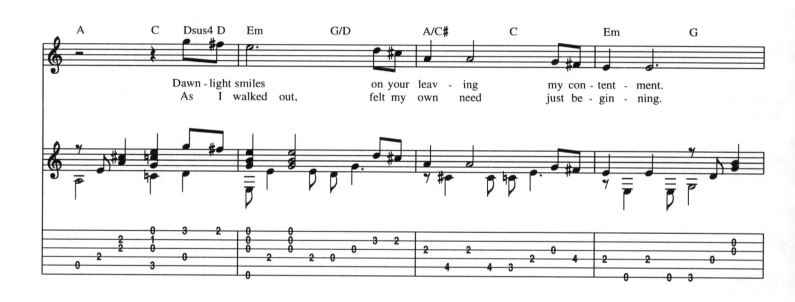

Dawn - light smiles   on your leav - ing   my con - tent - ment.
As I walked out,   felt my own need   just be - gin - ning.

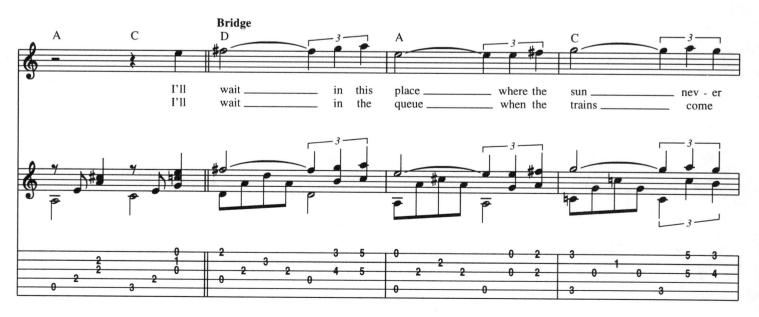

Bridge

I'll wait _____ in this place _____ where the sun _____ nev - er
I'll wait _____ in the queue _____ when the trains _____ come

shines;   wait _____ in this place _____ where the shad - ows
back,   lie _____ with you _____ where the shad - ows

1.
run   from them - selves. _____   2. You said
run   from them -   selves.

Outro

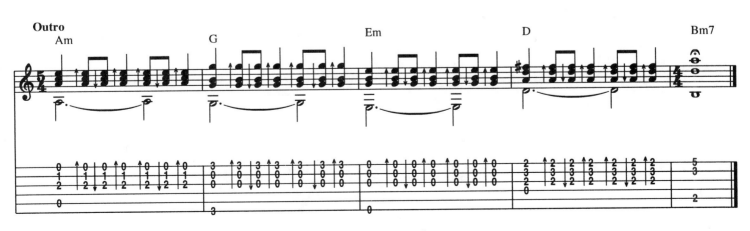

Wonderful Tonight

Words and Music by Eric Clapton

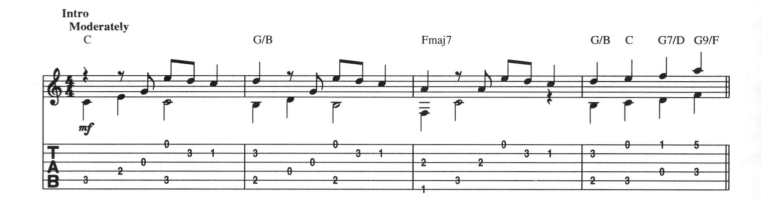